ANCIENT MARINE LIFE

LIVYATAN

BY KATE MOENING
ILLUSTRATIONS BY MAT EDWARDS

EPIC

BELLWETHER MEDIA • MINNEAPOLIS, MN

EPIC

EPIC BOOKS are no ordinary books. They burst with intense action, high-speed heroics, and shadows of the unknown. Are you ready for an Epic adventure?

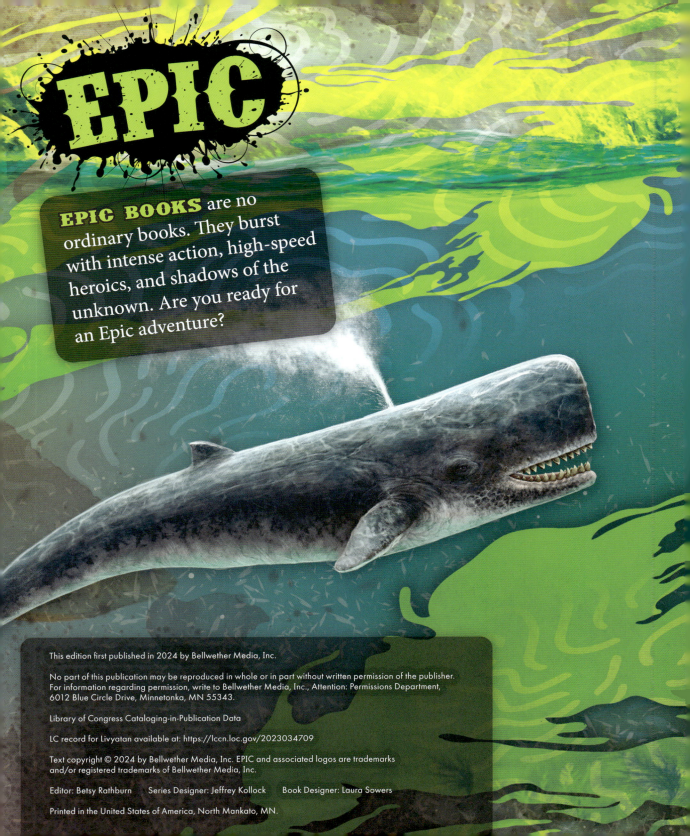

This edition first published in 2024 by Bellwether Media, Inc.

No part of this publication may be reproduced in whole or in part without written permission of the publisher. For information regarding permission, write to Bellwether Media, Inc., Attention: Permissions Department, 6012 Blue Circle Drive, Minnetonka, MN 55343.

Library of Congress Cataloging-in-Publication Data

LC record for Livyatan available at: https://lccn.loc.gov/2023034709

Text copyright © 2024 by Bellwether Media, Inc. EPIC and associated logos are trademarks and/or registered trademarks of Bellwether Media, Inc.

Editor: Betsy Rathburn   Series Designer: Jeffrey Kollock   Book Designer: Laura Sowers

Printed in the United States of America, North Mankato, MN.

TABLE OF CONTENTS

WHAT WAS THE LIVYATAN?	4
THE LIFE OF THE LIVYATAN	12
FOSSILS AND EXTINCTION	16
GET TO KNOW THE LIVYATAN	20
GLOSSARY	22
TO LEARN MORE	23
INDEX	24

WHAT WAS THE LIVYATAN?

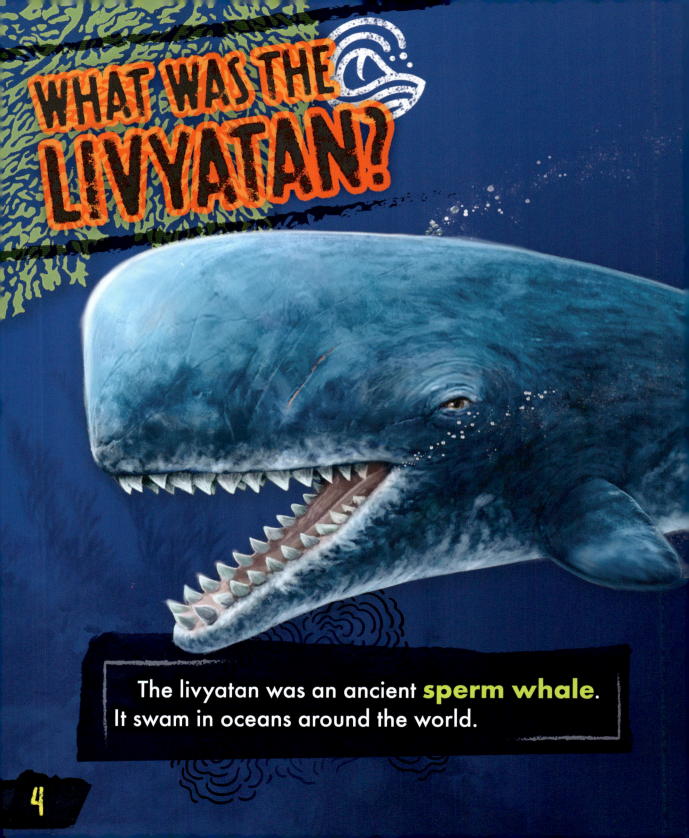

The livyatan was an ancient **sperm whale**. It swam in oceans around the world.

MAP OF THE WORLD

Neogene period

PRONUNCIATION

liv-YAH-tahn

It lived around 12 million years ago during the **Neogene period**. This was during the **Cenozoic era**.

The livyatan was a huge **mammal**. It grew around 60 feet (18.3 meters) long! Its head alone was almost 10 feet (3 meters) long.

It may have weighed over 60 tons (54 metric tons).

SIZE COMPARISON

about as long as two school buses

The livyatan had huge teeth. The biggest were around 12 inches (30 centimeters) long!

Its teeth were angled out. This helped it hang on to **prey**. Its wide mouth helped it bite down hard.

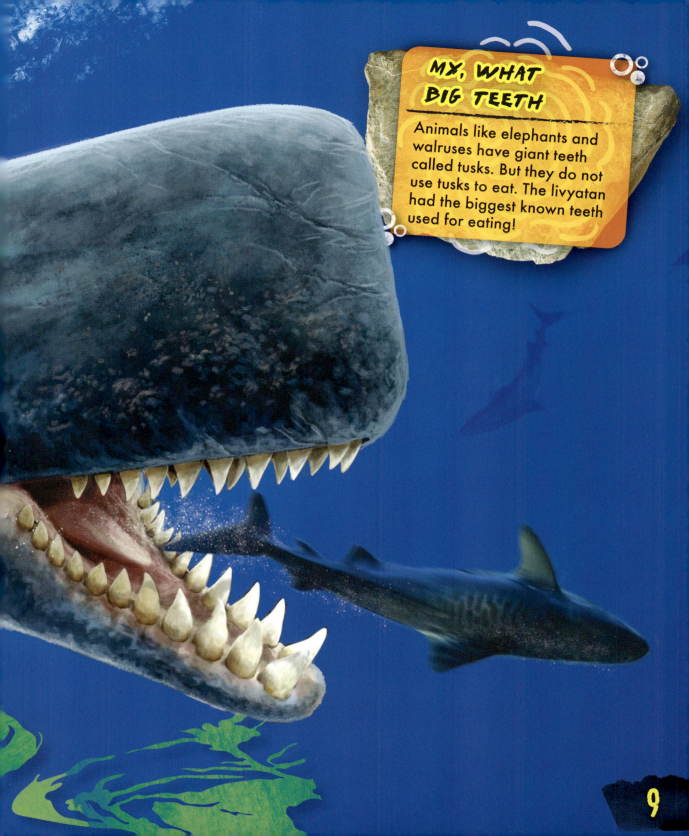

MY, WHAT BIG TEETH

Animals like elephants and walruses have giant teeth called tusks. But they do not use tusks to eat. The livyatan had the biggest known teeth used for eating!

The livyatan had a large head. It was filled with a waxy substance called **spermaceti**.

The livyatan could ram other animals during fights. Its head may have also helped with **echolocation**.

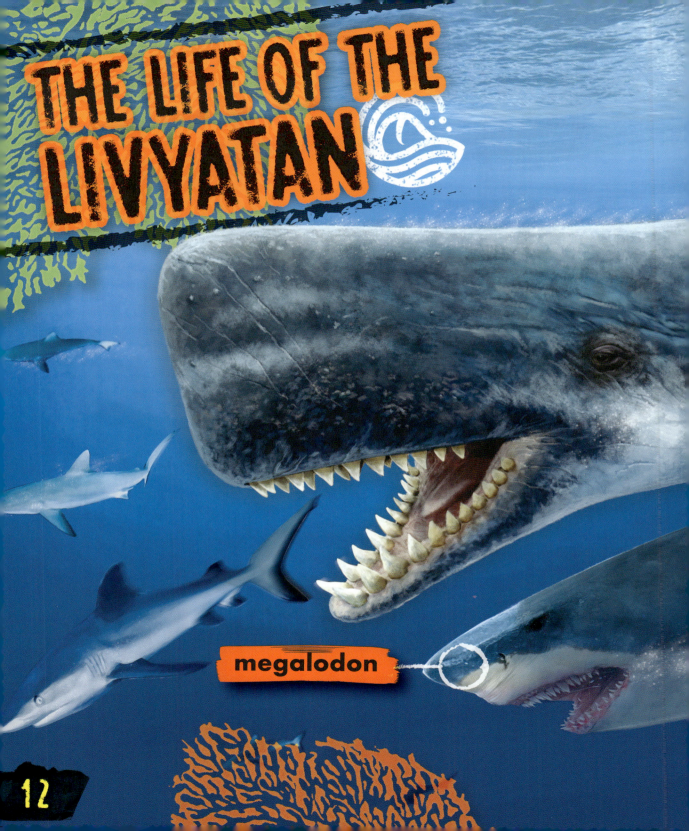

The livyatan was an **apex predator**. It mostly competed with the megalodon for food.

It ate sharks and other whales. It used echolocation to find meals. The sound could also **stun** prey!

LIVYATAN DIET

sharks

large fish

whales

The livyatan caught prey with its strong bite. Then it tore off big chunks of meat.

TEETH ALL OVER

Sperm whales today only have teeth on their bottom jaw. But the livyatan had both upper and lower teeth.

Babies were powerful **predators**, too! They may have eaten small whales and large fish.

Fossils and Extinction

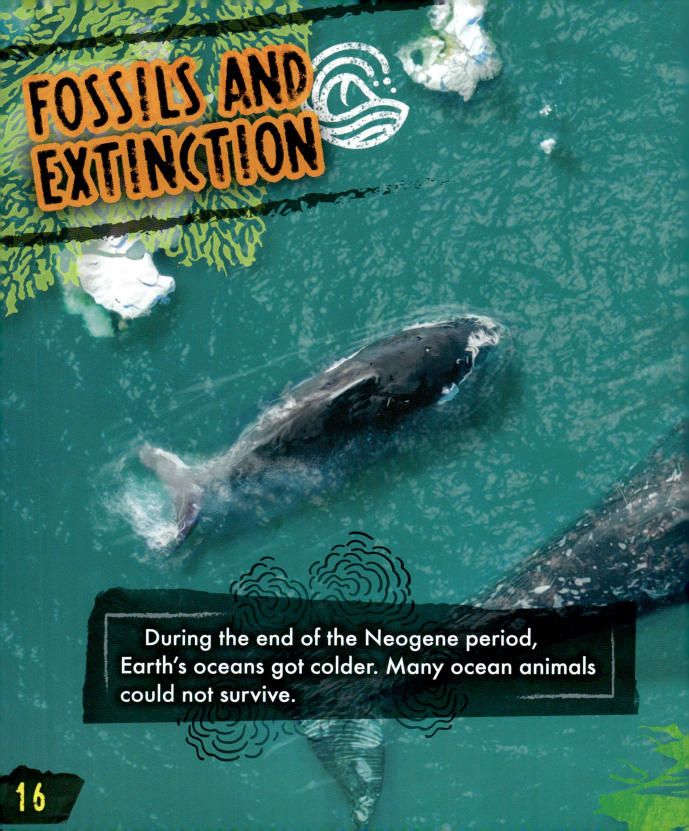

During the end of the Neogene period, Earth's oceans got colder. Many ocean animals could not survive.

The livyatan had less prey to hunt. It went **extinct**.

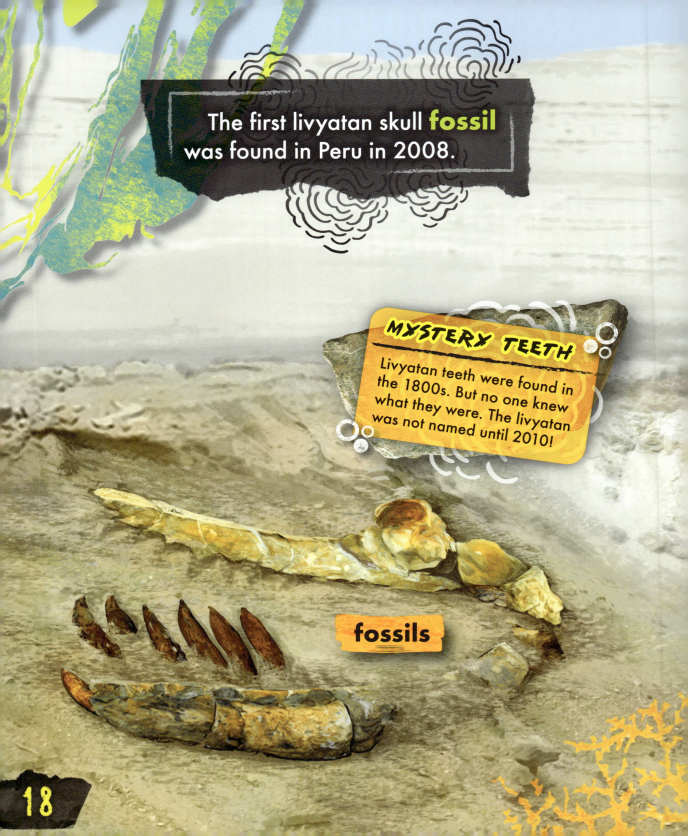

The first livyatan skull **fossil** was found in Peru in 2008.

MYSTERY TEETH

Livyatan teeth were found in the 1800s. But no one knew what they were. The livyatan was not named until 2010!

fossils

FIRST LIVYATAN SKULL FOSSIL FOUND

livyatan fossil cast

SOUTH AMERICA

FOUND in 2008

LOCATED Pisco Formation in Ica, Peru

Scientists have found more fossils since then. But the livyatan is still a new discovery. There is a lot to learn about this mighty whale!

GET TO KNOW THE LIVYATAN

LOCATION
oceans around the world

WEIGHT
over 60 tons
(54 metric tons)

FIRST FOSSILS FOUND
teeth in the 1800s

SIZE around 60 feet (18.3 meters) long

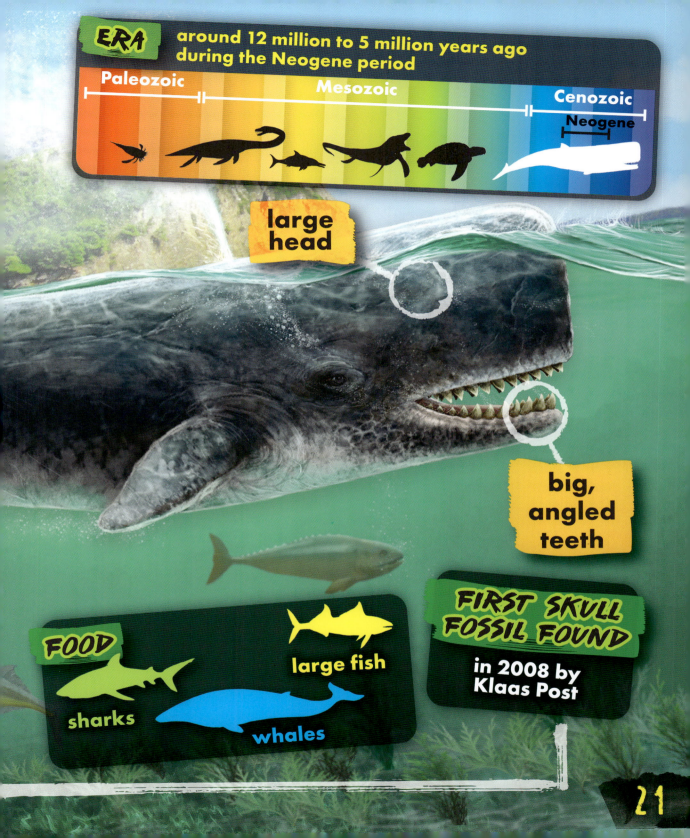

GLOSSARY

apex predator—an animal at the top of the food chain that is not preyed upon by other animals

Cenozoic era—a time in history that started 66 million years ago and continues to the present day

echolocation—a process for locating objects by using sound waves reflected back to the sender from the object

extinct—no longer living

fossil—the remains of a living thing that lived long ago

mammal—a warm-blooded animal that has a backbone and feeds its young milk

Neogene period—a time in history that happened about 23 million to 3 million years ago

predators—animals that hunt other animals for food

prey—animals that are hunted by other animals for food

sperm whale—a type of large, toothed whale with a huge head; sperm whale heads are filled with spermaceti.

spermaceti—a waxy, oily substance in the heads of sperm whales

stun—to cause something or someone to suddenly become very confused

TO LEARN MORE

AT THE LIBRARY

Moening, Kate. *Megalodon*. Minneapolis, Minn.: Bellwether Media, 2023.

Taylor, Charlotte. *Digging Up Sea Creature Fossils*. New York, N.Y.: Enslow Publishing, 2022.

Zoehfeld, Kathleen Weidner. *Prehistoric*. Greenbelt, Md.: What On Earth Books, 2019.

ON THE WEB

Factsurfer.com gives you a safe, fun way to find more information.

1. Go to www.factsurfer.com.

2. Enter "livyatan" into the search box and click 🔍.

3. Select your book cover to see a list of related content.

INDEX

apex predator, 13
babies, 15
bite, 8, 14
Cenozoic era, 5
Earth, 16
echolocation, 11, 13
extinct, 17
fights, 11
food, 13, 14, 15
fossil, 18, 19
get to know, 20–21
head, 6, 10, 11
mammal, 6
map, 5, 19

megalodon, 12, 13
name, 18
Neogene period, 5, 16
oceans, 4, 16
Peru, 18
predators, 15
prey, 8, 13, 14, 15, 17
pronunciation, 5
scientists, 19
size, 6, 7, 8, 9
skull, 18, 19
sperm whale, 4, 15
spermaceti, 10
teeth, 8, 9, 15, 18

The images in this book are reproduced through the courtesy of: Mat Edwards, front cover, pp. 1, 2-3, 4-5, 6-7, 8-9, 10-11, 12-13, 14-15, 16-17, 18-19, 20-21; Hectonichus/ Wikipedia, p. 19 (fossil); Wikipedia, p. 20 (fossil).